The Ultimate Comfort Food Cookbook

The Ultimate Comfort Food Cookbook

Jim Stephens

QuantumQuill Press

CONTENTS

A definitive Solace Food Cookbook

Welcome to an excursion through the inspiring universe of solace food, where every recipe isn't simply a pathway to delectable flavors yet a door to esteemed recollections and shared minutes. In "A definitive Solace Food Cookbook," we plunge profound into the dishes that calm the spirit, warm the heart, and take us back to a position of solace and happiness.

Meaning of Solace Food

Solace food, by its actual pith, is what could be compared to a warm embrace. The food brings out a feeling of home, having a place, and prosperity. These are the dishes we go to for comfort on a terrible day, celebrate with during life's achievements, and long for their irrefutable capacity to inspire our spirits. Solace food shifts broadly across societies and people, yet it generally shares the trait of being profoundly fulfilling and genuinely renewing.

The wizardry of solace food lies in its flavors as well as in its capacity to bring out recollections. Whether a basic bowl of chicken soup helps you to remember lighthearted youth days or a mind boggling family recipe went down through ages, solace food is about association — association with our past, to our friends and family, and to the minutes that characterize us.

The Close to home Association with Solace Food

The connection between solace food and our feelings runs profound. It's established in the brain science of taste and memory, where certain flavors and fragrances can quickly ship us to some other overall setting. This profound association makes solace food amazingly strong. It's about the actual demonstration of eating as well as about reproducing snapshots of euphoria, solace, and security.

Logical investigations have demonstrated the way that solace food can truly influence our state of mind, diminishing pressure and bringing out sensations of bliss. This is part of the way on the grounds that these food sources are in many cases wealthy in sugar, fat, and carbs, which can set off the mind's prize framework, and mostly in view of the individual and social importance these food sources hold for us.

What This Book Will Cover

In "A definitive Solace Food Cookbook," we will investigate the tremendous and changed scene of solace food, from the basic delights of heated merchandise to the generous fulfillment of stews and mains. Each segment of the book is devoted to a specific sort of solace food, giving a rich assortment of recipes that take care of various preferences and events.

•Soups and Stews: Dive into the mitigating warmth of custom made soups and stews that are ideally suited for crisp nights or when you're needing a soothing dinner.

•Heated Products: Find the delight of baking with recipes that fill your home with the powerful fragrance of new bread, treats, and biscuits.

•Generous Mains: Fulfill your appetite with satisfying primary dishes that reach from exemplary macaroni and cheddar to global top choices like lasagna and spread chicken.

•Breakfast Solaces: Begin your day right with consoling breakfast dishes that convince you to get up in the first part of the day.

•Global Solace Food sources: Take a culinary visit all over the planet with solace food sources from different societies, each with its own story and flavors.

Furthermore, we will investigate sound turns on exemplary solace food varieties, offering options for those hoping to partake in their #1 dishes in a lighter, more nutritious way.

Through "A definitive Solace Food Cookbook," we mean to praise the dishes that give us pleasure, solace, and a feeling of having a place. Whether you're a carefully prepared cook or beginning your culinary excursion, this book is a recognition for the widespread language of solace food — a language of affection, memory, and the straightforward delight of a decent feast.

1 |

The Science of Comfort Food

As we leave on this culinary excursion, understanding the basic study of solace food enhances our appreciation for these darling dishes. Solace food's ability to alleviate, elevate, and fulfill goes past simple taste — it connects with our mind, feelings, and recollections in complicated and captivating ways.

What Solace Food Means for the Cerebrum

Solace food varieties significantly affect the cerebrum's science, impacting mind-set and feelings. At the point when we eat food varieties high in starches, sugar, and fat, the mind discharges synapses like dopamine and serotonin. Dopamine, frequently alluded to as the "vibe great" synapse, assumes an essential part in the cerebrum's prize framework, creating sensations of joy and fulfillment. Serotonin, then again, is connected to prosperity and satisfaction, adding to a more quiet, more happy perspective.

The soothing impact of these food varieties is likewise connected with their capacity to diminish pressure related reactions in the body. Eating solace food can prompt a decrease in cortisol, the pressure chemical, assisting with lightening sensations of nervousness and stress. This physiological reaction is a key motivation behind why we naturally go after encouraging dishes in the midst of misery or while looking for comfort.

The Job of Wistfulness in Solace Food Inclinations

Sentimentality assumes a huge part in forming our solace food inclinations. Food sources that we partner with positive recollections, family customs, or social legacy frequently hold an extraordinary spot in our souls. These dishes are something beyond dinners; they are palatable associations with our past, bringing out recollections of friends and family, esteemed minutes, and a feeling of having a place.

The nostalgic force of solace food is well established in tangible memory. The taste, smell, and, surprisingly, the surface of specific food sources can set off clear memories. For instance, the smell of a pie baking in the stove could ship somebody back to their grandma's kitchen, remembering snapshots of affection and solace. This close to home association heightens the consoling impact of the food, making it an amazing asset for profound prosperity.

Solace Food Across Societies

While the idea of solace food is general, the dishes that inspire solace change broadly across societies. This variety mirrors the rich embroidered artwork of worldwide culinary customs and the various fixings and flavors esteemed by each culture.

In the US, solace food could incorporate works of art like macaroni and cheddar or fruity dessert. In Italy, it very well may be a generous bowl of pasta or a hand crafted pizza. In Japan, solace could emerge out of a warming bowl of ramen or a bento box loaded up with natural top picks. Each dish recounts an account of social character, family customs, and individual recollections, featuring the all inclusive requirement for solace and the different ways it very well may be accomplished through food.

This investigation of solace food across societies not just grandstands the range of dishes that bring individuals solace yet in addition underlines the consistent ideas that join us. Notwithstanding social contrasts, the quest for solace, delight, and a feeling of having a place through food is an all inclusive encounter.

2

Soups and Stews

Nothing epitomizes solace food very like a hot bowl of soup or stew. These dishes are supporting and warming as well as flexible and wealthy ever. Beneath, we present a choice of recipes that reach from revered works of art to current bends, each encouraging to convey solace in each spoonful.

Exemplary Chicken Noodle Soup

•Serves: 6

•Fixings:

o2 tablespoons olive oil

o1 huge onion, cleaved

o3 carrots, stripped and cut

o2 celery stems, cut

o2 garlic cloves, minced

o8 cups chicken stock

o2 straight leaves

o½ teaspoon dried thyme

oSalt and pepper to taste

o2 cups cooked chicken, destroyed (ideally bosom or thigh)

o8 oz egg noodles

o2 tablespoons new parsley, cleaved

•Directions:

1. In a huge pot, heat the olive oil over medium intensity. Add the onion, carrots, and celery. Cook, blending incidentally, until the vegetables are mellowed, around 5 minutes.
2. Add the garlic and cook for one more moment until fragrant.
3. Pour in the chicken stock and add the cove leaves and thyme. Season with salt and pepper. Heat to the point of boiling, then decrease intensity and stew for 20 minutes.
4. Add the destroyed chicken and egg noodles. Cook as per the noodle bundle guidelines, or until the noodles are delicate.
5. Remove the inlet leaves and change preparing if important. Mix in the new parsley not long prior to serving.

•Individual Touch: For a heartier rendition, you can add diced potatoes with the carrots and celery. In the event that you're searching for a sans gluten choice, substitute egg noodles with your number one sans gluten pasta or rice.

Generous Meat Stew

•Serves: 6

•Fixings:

o2 pounds hamburger hurl, cut into 1-inch shapes

o¼ cup regular baking flour

oSalt and pepper to taste

o3 tablespoons olive oil, isolated

o1 onion, slashed

o3 carrots, stripped and cut

o3 potatoes, stripped and cubed

o2 celery stems, cut

o4 cups meat stock

o1 teaspoon dried rosemary
o1 teaspoon dried thyme
o2 tablespoons tomato glue
o1 cup frozen peas
•Guidelines:

1. Season the hamburger solid shapes with salt and pepper, then, at that point, throw them with flour to cover.
2. In an enormous pot, heat 2 tablespoons of olive oil over medium-high intensity. Add the hamburger in bunches, carmelizing on all sides. Eliminate the meat and put away.
3. In a similar pot, add the excess tablespoon of olive oil. Add the onion, carrots, and celery. Cook until the vegetables begin to relax, around 5 minutes.
4. Return the meat to the pot. Add potatoes, hamburger stock, rosemary, thyme, and tomato glue. Mix well to join.
5. Bring to a bubble, then diminish intensity, cover, and stew for around 90 minutes, or until the meat is delicate.
6. Add the frozen peas and cook for an additional 10 minutes. Change preparing to taste.

•Individual Touch: For a more extravagant flavor, you can add a sprinkle of red wine with the meat stock. In the event that you favor a thicker stew, blend 2 tablespoons of flour in with ¼ cup of water and add to the stew during the most recent 30 minutes of cooking.

These recipes are a beginning stage, catching the quintessence of solace that soups and stews offer of real value. Every recipe in this segment is intended to be versatile, considering personalization in view of dietary requirements, individual preferences, or accessible fixings.

As we continue with the cookbook, impending segments will incorporate Prepared Products, Good Mains, Breakfast Solaces, and Global Solace Food varieties, each loaded up with recipes that guarantee to convey solace and fulfillment.

Assuming you have explicit recipes, varieties, or dietary contemplations you might want to find in the impending segments, if it's not too much trouble, let me know. This cookbook is a cooperative exertion, pointed toward making an assortment that resounds with all who look for solace in the kitchen.

3

Baked Goods

The smell of organized stock filling the kitchen is totally possibly of the most easing and welcoming sensation. This piece of "A decisive Solace Food Cookbook" is centered around people who track down comfort in the sparkle of the broiler and bliss in the improvement of something sweet or magnificent with no preparation. Here, we acclaim the undying allure of baking with three quintessential recipes: Honorable Chocolate Chip Treats, Privately constructed Bread, and Blueberry Rolls.

Admirable Chocolate Chip Treats

•Yield: Around 24 treats

•Decorations:

o1 cup (2 sticks) unsalted spread, mellowed

o¾ cup granulated sugar

o¾ cup stuffed normal concealed sugar

o1 teaspoon vanilla concentrate

o2 huge eggs

o2 ¼ cups standard flour

o1 teaspoon baking pop

o½ teaspoon salt

o2 cups semisweet chocolate chips
o1 cup hacked nuts (discretionary)
•Headings:

1. Preheat your stove to 375°F (190°C). Line baking sheets with material paper.
2. In a huge bowl, cream together the spread, granulated sugar, regular concealed sugar, and vanilla concentrate until smooth and cushioned. Beat in the eggs, individually, it are completely cemented to guarantee they.
3. In another bowl, whisk together the flour, baking pop, and salt. Bit by bit beat the dry decorations into the spread blend as of in the no so distant past consolidated. Mix in the chocolate chips and nuts, if utilizing.
4. Drop mix by switched tablespoonfuls onto the set around baking sheets, giving space for the treats to spread.
5. Bake for 9 to 11 minutes, or until the treats are magnificent brown around the edges yet at the same time delicate in the middle. Grant them to cool on the baking sheet for 5 minutes prior to moving to wire racks to totally cool.

•Individual Touch: For chewier treats, make a pass at overriding one cup of standard flour with bread flour. Endeavor different things with various blend ins like white chocolate chips, dried cranberries, or coconut parts of make these treats your own.

Privately constructed Bread

•Yield: 1 section

•Decorations:

o3 cups typical baking flour, as well as something else for cleaning
o1 pack (¼ ounce) dynamic dry yeast
o1 teaspoon salt

o1 tablespoon sugar
o1 ¼ cups warm water (around 110°F or 45°C)
o2 tablespoons olive oil
•Headings:

1. In a colossal bowl, consolidate the flour, yeast, salt, and sugar. Add the warm water and olive oil, and mix until a shaggy player structures.
2. Turn the player out onto a floured surface and work until smooth and adaptable, something like 10 minutes. Place the player in a lubed bowl, cover with a sodden surface, and permit it to ascend in a warm spot until copied in size, something like 60 minutes.
3. Punch down the hitter and shape it into a piece. Place it in a lubed 9x5 inch fragment dish. Cover and let rise again until copied, around 30 minutes.
4. Preheat your barbecue to 375°F (190°C). Heat the bread for 25 to 30 minutes, or until the piece is marvelous brown and sounds void when tapped on the base. Cool in the journey for gold minutes, then, at that point, turn out onto a wire rack to totally cool.

•Individual Touch: For a trademark flavor, blend in entire wheat flour for up to half of the typical flour. Add flavors like rosemary or thyme, or seeds like sunflower or pumpkin, for a heavenly turn.

Blueberry Rolls
•Yield: 12 rolls
•Decorations:
o2 cups standard flour
o½ cup sugar
o3 teaspoons baking powder

o½ teaspoon salt

o¾ cup milk

o1/3 cup vegetable oil

o1 egg

o1 cup new or frozen blueberries

•Headings:

1. Preheat your stove to 400°F (200°C). Line a bread roll tin with paper liners or oil the cups.
2. In an epic bowl, join the flour, sugar, baking powder, and salt. In another bowl, whisk together the milk, oil, and egg. Mix the wet decorations into the evaporate decorations to this point drenched. Get over in the blueberries.
3. Fill the set up bread roll cups around 66% full. Plan for 20 to 25 minutes, or until a toothpick introduced into the mark of intermingling of a roll concedes all.
4. Let the bread rolls cool in the chance minutes going before moving them to a wire rack to totally cool.

•Individual Touch: Add a streusel outflanking going before baking for additional exquisiteness and surface. Join as one ½ cup of flour, ¼ cup of sugar, and ¼ cup of spread until delicate, then, sprinkle over the roll hitter.

These recipes go probably as the establishment for the "Organized Things" area, offering honorable solace in each eat. As we progress through the cookbook, we'll look at additional recipes, each with its wonderful story and grouping to guarantee there's something for each cake educated authority, paying little mind to limit level or inclination.

Then, we'll advance forward to "Liberal Mains," where the consoling hug of warmed things gives way to the wonderful meaning of full eats expected to gather families around the supper table. Tolerating that there are express dishes or baking tips you ought to see related with the last understanding of this part, empathetically express your impressions.

4

Hearty Mains

Macaroni and Cheddar
•Serves: 6-8
•Trimmings:
o1 pound elbow macaroni
o4 cups obliterated sharp cheddar
o2 cups milk
o2 tablespoons customary flour
o4 tablespoons unsalted spread
o½ teaspoon paprika
oSalt and pepper to taste
o½ cup breadcrumbs (for fixing)
•Headings:

1. Preheat your oven to 350°F (175°C). Oil a 9x13 inch baking dish.
2. Cook the macaroni according to package rules until still fairly firm. Channel and set aside.
3. In a pot, melt the spread over medium power. Blend in the flour to make a roux, cooking for 1-2 minutes until bubbly.

Gradually race in the milk, ensuring no bunches structure. Cook until the mix thickens and is smooth.

4. Remove from force, and blend in 3 cups of cheddar until relaxed. Add paprika, salt, and pepper. Merge the cheddar sauce with the drained macaroni, then, at that point, move to the set up baking dish. Sprinkle the abundance cheddar and breadcrumbs over the top.

5. Bake for 25-30 minutes, or until the top is splendid brown and bubbly.

•Individual Touch: Work on your macaroni and cheddar with increases like cooked bacon, diced tomatoes, or sautéed mushrooms. For a fiery kick, mix in some diced jalapeños or a bit of hot sauce.

Meatloaf

•Serves: 6

•Trimmings:

o1 ½ pounds ground meat

o1 egg, beaten

o1 onion, finely hacked

o1 cup milk

o1 cup dried bread pieces

oSalt and pepper to taste

o2 tablespoons hearty shaded sugar

o2 tablespoons mustard

o⅓ cup ketchup

•Headings:

1. Preheat your oven to 350°F (175°C).

2. In a colossal bowl, join as one the ground meat, egg, onion, milk, and bread scraps. Season with salt and pepper. Place the

mix into a gently lubed 5x9 inch segment compartment, or design it into a piece and spot it in a baking dish.

3. In a little bowl, join the gritty hued sugar, mustard, and ketchup. Mix well and pour over the meatloaf.

4. Bake for 1 hour or until the meatloaf is cooked through and the juices run clear. Permit it to rest for 10 minutes preceding cutting.

•Individual Touch: For a more delectable outside, add a covering of barbecue sauce or a mix of ketchup and Worcestershire sauce at this point of baking. Mix different meats like pork and burger for a moved flavor profile.

Chicken Pot Pie

•Serves: 6

•Trimmings:

o1 pound skinless, boneless chicken chest parts - cubed

o1 cup cut carrots

o1 cup frozen green peas

o½ cup cut celery

o⅓ cup margarine

o⅓ cup cut onion

o⅓ cup standard flour

o½ teaspoon salt

o¼ teaspoon dim pepper

o¼ teaspoon celery seed

o1 ¾ cups chicken stock

o⅔ cup milk

o2 (9 inch) unbaked pie structures

•Headings:

1. Preheat oven to 425°F (220°C).

2. In a pot, unite chicken, carrots, peas, and celery. Add water to cover and rise for 15 minutes. Wipe out from force, channel, and set aside.

3. In comparable pot, cook onions in spread over medium force until sensitive and clear. Blend in flour, salt, pepper, and celery seed. Progressively blend in chicken stock and milk. Stew over medium-low power until thick. Take out from force and set aside.

4. Place one pie covering in the lower part of a pie holder. Pour the chicken mix on top, then pour the hot liquid mix over. Cover with the resulting pie outside, seal the edges, and eliminate excess hitter. Make a couple of little slices in the top to allow steam to move away.

5. Bake for 30 to 35 minutes, or until cake is splendid brown and filling is bubbly. Cool for 10 minutes preceding serving.

•Individual Touch: Examination with different vegetables according to prepare or tendency, similar to mushrooms, corn, or potatoes. A sprinkle of flavors like thyme or rosemary can add significance to the flavor.

These "Great Mains" are expected to satisfy and comfort, giving a foundation whereupon to build an assortment of fulfilling dishes that convey warmth to any table. As we progress, we'll examine more groupings, ensuring a rich combination of flavors and customs are tended to in "A conclusive Comfort Food Cookbook."

Resulting stages consolidate covering "Breakfast Comforts" and "Worldwide Comfort Food sources," where we'll dive into the enhancing start of the day and examine how different social orders unravel comfort food. If there are explicit dishes or additional parts you should coordinate into these or past fragments, your input will help with trim this cookbook into a thorough manual for comfort food.

5

Breakfast Comforts

Hotcakes
•Serves: 4
•Trimmings:
o1 ½ cups standard flour
o3 ½ teaspoons baking powder
o1 teaspoon salt
o1 tablespoon white sugar
o1 ¼ cups milk
o1 egg
o3 tablespoons broke up margarine
oAdditional spread for cooking
•Rules:

1. In a gigantic bowl, channel together the flour, baking powder, salt, and sugar. Make a well in the center and pour in the milk, egg, and broke up margarine; mix until smooth.
2. Heat a delicately oiled iron or frying pan over medium-extreme focus. Pour or scoop the player onto the iron, using

approximately 1/4 cup for each pancake. Brown on the different sides and serve hot.

•Individual Touch: For an extra twist, wrinkle in new blueberries, chocolate chips, or gently cut bananas into the hitter preceding cooking. For a lighter, fluffier surface, separate the egg, beat the white to strong zeniths, and cross-over it into the hitter last.

French Toast

•Serves: 4

•Trimmings:

o8 thick cuts of bread (brioche or challah work perfectly)

o4 eggs

o1 cup milk

o2 teaspoons vanilla concentrate

o1 teaspoon ground cinnamon

o¼ cup spread

oMaple syrup, for serving

•Bearings:

1. In a gigantic bowl, whisk together eggs, milk, vanilla concentrate, and cinnamon.

2. Heat a gigantic skillet or iron over medium force and condense a piece of the margarine.

3. Dip each cut of bread in the egg mix, allowing it to drench on each side. Place the soaked bread cuts onto the hot skillet and cook until splendid brown on the different sides.

4. Serve hot with maple syrup.

•Individual Touch: Examination with the egg blend by adding a sprinkle of orange liquor or subbing a piece of the milk with significant cream for a more extreme craving. Top with powdered sugar, new berries, or a touch of whipped cream for an extra phenomenal touch.

Omelets

•Serves: 1

•Trimmings:

o3 eggs

o1 tablespoon water

oSalt and pepper to taste

o1 tablespoon margarine

oFillings: cheddar, diced ham, sautéed mushrooms, cut spinach, diced ring peppers, or any blend thereof

•Rules:

1. In a bowl, beat the eggs with water, salt, and pepper.
2. Heat margarine in a non-stick skillet over medium force until hot. Pour in the egg blend. As eggs set at the edges, with a spatula, gently push cooked portions close to the center, moving the skillet to allow uncooked eggs to stream into void spaces.
3. When the eggs are set and no evident liquid egg remains, put the filling on one side of the omelet. Wrinkle the omelet in half with the spatula and slide it onto a plate.

•Individual Touch: The omelet is an optimal material for imagination. Have a go at adding new flavors, a sprinkle of your #1 cheddar, or a blend of additional items from dinner for a novel and individual breeze. For a woolen omelet, add a little sprinkle of cream to the eggs before beating.

These morning feast recipes typify the essence of morning comfort, giving a warm and inviting starting to rapidly. They offer a blend of straightforwardness and adaptability, ensuring that there's something for each taste and occasion.

Pushing ahead, the accompanying section, "Overall Comfort Food sources," will research the overall perspective on comfort food, showing how different social orders track down solace and get a kick out of their culinary traditions. If there are unequivocal breakfast dishes or assortments you acknowledge would upgrade this part further, your thoughts are reliably welcome.

6

International Comfort Foods

Italian Lasagna
•Serves: 8
•Decorations:
o1 pound sweet Italian straight to the point
o¾ pound lean ground meat
o½ cup minced onion
o2 cloves garlic, squashed
o1 (28 ounce) can squashed tomatoes
o2 (6 ounce) compartments tomato stick
o2 (6.5 ounce) compartments canned pureed tomatoes
o½ cup water
o2 tablespoons white sugar
o1 ½ teaspoons dried basil leaves
o½ teaspoon fennel seeds
o1 teaspoon Italian flavoring
o1 tablespoon salt
o¼ teaspoon ground faint pepper
o4 tablespoons cut new parsley
o12 lasagna noodles

o16 ounces ricotta cheddar
o1 egg
o¾ teaspoon salt
o¾ pound mozzarella cheddar, cut
o¾ cup ground Parmesan cheddar
•Headings:

1. In a Dutch stove, cook hotdog, ground burger, onion, and garlic over medium power until particularly sautéed. Mix in squashed tomatoes, tomato stick, pureed tomatoes, and water. Season with sugar, basil, fennel seeds, Italian improving, 1 tablespoon salt, pepper, and 2 tablespoons parsley. Stew, covered, for around 1 ½ hours, blending startlingly.
2. Bring a huge pot of painstakingly salted water to an air pocket. Cook lasagna noodles in permeating water for 8 to 10 minutes. Channel noodles, and flush with cold water.
3. In a blending bowl, join ricotta cheddar with egg, remaining parsley, and ¾ teaspoon salt.
4. Preheat broiler to 375°F (190°C).
5. To collect, spread 1 ½ cups of meat sauce in the lower some part of a 9x13 inch baking dish. Coordinate 6 noodles the long far over meat sauce. Spread with one piece of the ricotta cheddar blend. Top with 33% of mozzarella cheddar cuts. Spoon 1 ½ cups meat sauce over mozzarella, and sprinkle with ¼ cup Parmesan cheddar. Repeat layers, and top with phenomenal mozzarella and Parmesan cheddar.
6. Cover with foil: to forestall remaining, either give foil cooking sprinkle, or assurance the foil doesn't contact the cheddar.
7. Bake in preheated barbecue for 25 minutes. Crash foil, and force 25 extra minutes. Cool for 15 minutes going before serving.

•Individual Touch: Consider adding a layer of cooked spinach or mushrooms to the lasagna for an additional serving of vegetables. For a lighter translation, use ground turkey or chicken rather than cheeseburger and frankfurter.

Indian Spread Chicken

•Serves: 4-6

•Decorations:

o1 ½ pounds chicken chest, cut into scaled down pieces

o1 tablespoon lemon juice

o1 teaspoon turmeric powder

o2 teaspoons garam masala, secluded

o2 teaspoons ground cumin, secluded

o1 tablespoon ginger garlic stick

oSalt to taste

o¼ cup unsalted spread

o1 onion, finely hacked

o1 (14 ounce) might tomato whenever puree

o1 cup significant cream

o1 tablespoon sugar

o¼ cup water (if essential)

oFresh cilantro for enhance

•Rules:

1. Marinate the chicken with lemon juice, turmeric, 1 teaspoon garam masala, 1 teaspoon cumin, ginger garlic glue, and salt. License it to sit for some place close to 1 hour or transient in the cooler.

2. Heat margarine in an immense skillet over medium power. Add the onions and cook until delicate and clear. Add the marinated chicken and cook until the outside is carefully sautéed.

3. Stir in the tomato puree, remaining garam masala, and cumin. Cook for a few minutes until the tomato lessens decently.

4. Lower the power and add the cream and sugar. Stew for 10-15 minutes, adding a little water in the event that the sauce gets pointlessly thick.

5. Garnish with new cilantro prior to serving. Present with rice or naan bread.

•Individual Touch: For a veggie darling variety, substitute chicken with tofu and use coconut milk instead of huge cream. Adding a hint of fenugreek leaves can overhaul the flavor fundamentally.

Japanese Ramen

•Serves: 4

•Decorations:

o4 cups chicken or vegetable stock

o2 cups water

o2 packs second ramen noodles (arranging bundles disposed of)

o1 tablespoon soy sauce

o1 tablespoon miso stick (discretionary)

o2 teaspoons sesame oil

o½ pound cut cooked pork abdomen or chicken

o4 delicate frothed eggs, stripped and divided

o1 cup cut green onion

o1 cup new spinach

o1 cup cut mushrooms

oBamboo shoots, ocean improvement sheets, and sesame seeds for decorate

•Course:

1. In a colossal pot, heat the stock and water with the possible consequence of foaming. Add soy sauce, miso stick (if utilizing), and sesame oil. Diminish the ability to stew.
2. Add the ramen noodles and cook as indicated by bundle rules, regularly 3-4 minutes.
3. Divide the noodles into bowls. Top with pork stomach or chicken, delicate frothed eggs, green onions, spinach, and mushrooms.
4. Pour the hot stock over the top. Decorate with bamboo shoots, ocean advancement, and sesame seeds.

•Individual Touch: Change your ramen bowl with your #1 decorations, for example, corn, bean sprouts, or bok choy. For a super hot kick, add a spot of bean stew glue or cuts of jalapeño.

These overall dishes incorporate the adaptability and rich kinds of solace food from around the world. Every recipe offers a window into the culinary practices that have passed solace on to boundless ages, welcoming you to explore new friendly orders and tastes right from your kitchen.

Then, we will close our excursion with a segment focused areas of strength for on commendable solace food sources, giving choices to those needing to partake in their top picks in a more nutritious way. Your snippets of data and propensities will keep on planning the improvement of this cookbook, promising it changes into a valued wellspring of solace and motivation.

7

Healthy Twists on Classic Comfort Foods

Subbing Elements for Better Adaptations

The way to making better variants of your number one solace food varieties lies in smart replacements that upgrade dietary benefit without compromising taste. Here are a few general techniques:

•Utilize Entire Grains: Supplant white pasta, bread, and rice with entire grain choices. Entire grains give more fiber, which can assist you with feeling full longer and proposition a scope of medical advantages.

•Lean Proteins: Decide on more slender cuts of meat, like chicken bosom or turkey, and integrate plant-based proteins like beans and lentils to decrease fat admission while keeping the dishes good.

•Increment Vegetables: Amp up the vegetable substance in any dish for added supplements, fiber, and volume. This makes dinners more nutritious as well as more bright and delightful.

•Sound Fats: Substitute spread and cream with better fats like olive oil and avocados. In baking, unsweetened fruit purée or crushed bananas can supplant oil or spread.

•Lessen Sugar: Cut back on sugar in recipes or utilize regular sugars like honey, maple syrup, or pureed natural products to improve sweets and heated merchandise.

Lighter Adaptations of Weighty Works of art

Applying the above techniques, how about we reproduce three exemplary solace food sources into lighter, better forms without forfeiting their spirit relieving claim.

Eased Up Macaroni and Cheddar

•Fixings:

oWhole-grain or vegetable based pasta

oLow-fat milk

oA blend of sharp cheddar and butternut squash puree for the sauce

oA fixing of entire grain breadcrumbs blended in with olive oil

•Contort: The butternut squash puree adds smoothness and a healthful lift to the cheddar sauce, considering less cheddar and milk use. The entire grain pasta and breadcrumb beating increment the fiber content, making this dish seriously filling and nutritious.

Better Meatloaf

•Fixings:

oLean ground turkey or a blend of lean meat and lentils

oWhole-grain breadcrumbs

oPureed vegetables (carrots, onions, and ringer peppers) blended into the portion

oA coat produced using diminished sugar ketchup and balsamic vinegar

•Wind: Consolidating lean meats, lentils, and vegetables diminishes fat as well as upgrades the portion's dampness and flavor. The entire grain breadcrumbs add fiber, and the better coating choice lessens sugar content.

Taken apart Chicken Pot Pie

•Fixings:

oGrilled or prepared chicken bosom, prepared with spices

oA mixture of steamed or simmered vegetables (carrots, peas, potatoes, and onions)

oA sauce produced using low-fat milk thickened with a touch of entire wheat flour

oWhole-grain bread rolls or a light puff baked good fixing

•Wind: This dismantled methodology keeps up with the quintessence of chicken pot pie yet fundamentally lessens calories and fat by disposing of the conventional pie outside layer and utilizing a lighter sauce. Serving the parts independently or as a layered meal considers the soothing flavors to radiate through in a better configuration.

Changing exemplary solace food sources into better forms is a craftsmanship that offsets sustenance with flavor. These models delineate that with a couple of imaginative changes, you can partake in your #1 solace dishes such that's better for your body yet at the same time fulfills your spirit.

As we wrap up this part, recollect that good dieting doesn't mean forfeiting the food sources you love. About pursuing more brilliant decisions line up with a fair way of life. The last segment of our cookbook will give an outline and shutting considerations, integrating our process through solace food with an accentuation on assortment, balance, and the delight of cooking. Assuming that there are any more unambiguous dishes or ideas you might want to investigate, go ahead and let me know.

Conclusion

As we arrive at the last pages of "A definitive Solace Food Cookbook," now is the right time to consider the excursion we've left upon together — an excursion through the warm, welcoming universe of solace food. From the primary spoonful of a good soup to the last chomp of a sweet treat, solace food has the remarkable ability to summon recollections, give pleasure, and proposition comfort. This cookbook has crossed societies and cooking styles, exhibiting how the widespread language of solace food rises above borders and joins all of us.

Recap of the Significance of Solace Food

Solace food is considerably more than just food; it's an encounter, a memory, and a sense that everything is safe and secure and warmth. The dinners help us to remember home, take us back to esteemed minutes, and cause us to feel really focused on. All through this cookbook, we've investigated the science behind solace food — what it means for the cerebrum, the profound associations we produce with specific dishes, and how these inclinations are impacted by culture and individual history. We've dug into recipes that range the range from soups and stews to prepared products, good mains, and global top choices, each with its own story and spot in the realm of solace cooking.

Consolation to Try different things with Recipes and Track down Private Solace in Cooking

The recipes introduced in this cookbook are something beyond directions; they are solicitations to investigate, adjust, and make. Cooking is an individual excursion, one that permits you to articulate your thoughts, try different things with flavors, and find what really brings you solace. We urge you to take these recipes and make them your own — change out fixings in light of what you love or what you have close by, attempt new procedures, and don't hesitate for even a moment to come up short. It's all important for the culinary experience.

Keep in mind, solace food isn't just about enjoying the natural yet additionally about finding new top choices and making your own customs. Whether it's putting a sound curve on an exemplary dish, investigating global cooking styles, or essentially consummating your flapjack flip, the demonstration of preparing and sharing food can give colossal pleasure and fulfillment.

Shutting Contemplations

As you close this book and head into the kitchen, recollect that solace food is about something other than the actual food — it's about the solace, love, and recollections that accompany it. It's tied in with get-together around the table with friends and family, sharing stories and chuckling, and sustaining our bodies as well as our spirits.

"A definitive Solace Food Cookbook" was made to rouse, to comfort, and to give somewhat more pleasure into your cooking and your life. May these recipes act as a beginning stage for endless feasts and recollections to come. Here's to tracking down solace, each dish in turn.

Much obliged to you for going along with us on this flavorful excursion. May your kitchen forever be loaded up with the smells of solace, and may every dinner carry you nearer to those you share it with. Blissful cooking!

www.ingramcontent.com/pod-product-compliance
Lightning Source LLC
Chambersburg PA
CBHW021405160726
47994CB00007B/3086